MW01559542

THIS BOOK

belongs to:

CPSIA information can be obtained
at www.ICGtesting.com
Printed in the USA
LVHW081254031222
734520LV00013B/717

9 781710 367294